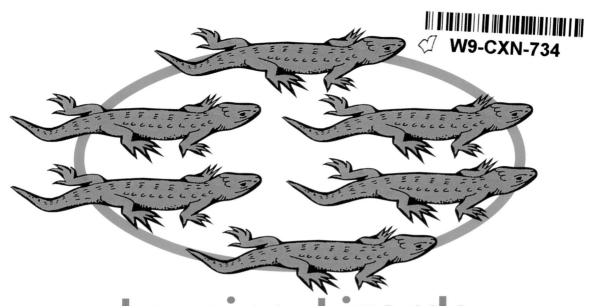

Leaping Lizards

by Charlotte Stadler

Table of Contents

What Do We Need to Play Our Game?

Our teacher told us that we were going to play a game in math today. We were very happy! She showed us the game board.

Then she showed us the other things
we would need to play the game.

There were 12 lizards.

There were
two number cubes.

One was green
and one was red.

What Is on the Number Cubes?

My friend picked up the number cubes. She looked at them and turned them all around. She said that each cube had six sides. She said that there were dots on each side.

What is the smallest number
you could get if you added the dots
on one green cube and one red cube?

What is the largest number you could get?

How Do We Play Our Game?

Our teacher put the 12 lizards on the game board at the starting line.

The lizard that leaped to the finish line first would be the winner.

Our teacher said that we should
take turns rolling the number cubes.

The number we get when we add up the
dots will tell us which lizard can leap
ahead one space.

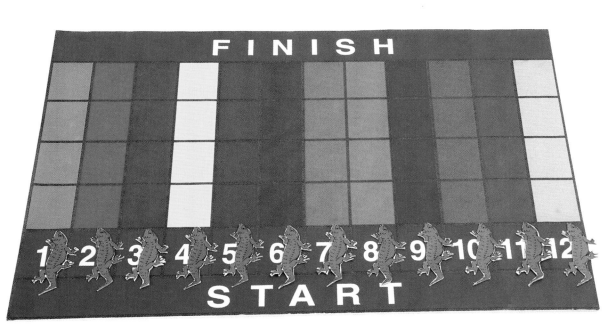

What Happened When We Played Our Game?

My friend went first. She rolled the number cubes.

This is what she rolled.

$$5 + 1 = 6$$

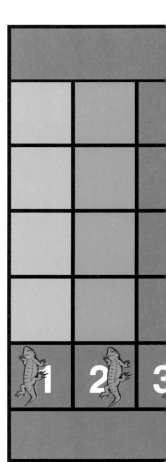

Which lizard do you think she moved?

This is what our game board looked like when we were finished.

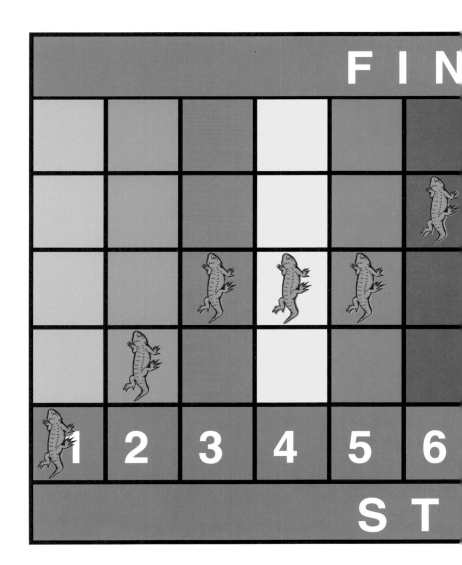

Which lizard won?
Which lizard came in second?
Which lizard came in third?
Which lizard never leaped?

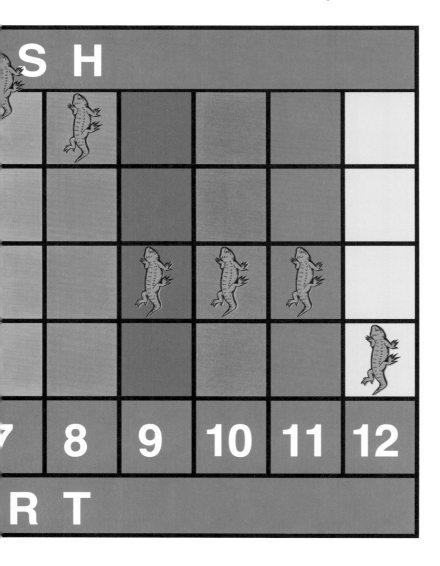

Our teacher asked us to play the game again. This time she told us to write down our number sentences in the spaces instead of moving the lizards.

FINISH

$2+4=$

$5+1=$

$4+1=5$ $4+2=$

$2+2=4$ $2+3=5$ $3+3=6$

$1+1=2$ $2+1=3$ $1+3=4$ $3+2=5$ $2+4=$

1 2 3 4 5 6

START

This is what our game board looked like when we finished.

Which lizard came in first this time?

+4=7					
2+5=7	5+3=8				
4+3=7	2+6=8	5+4=9	4+6=10		
6+1=7	4+4=8	3+6=9	5+5=10	6+5=11	6+6=12
7	8	9	10	11	12

What Did We Learn After Playing Our Game Many Times?

Look at this table we made
after playing our game many times.
It shows all the different ways
we could roll the number cubes to make
each lizard leap.

1	2	3	4	5	6
	1+1=2	1+2=3	1+3=4	1+4=5	1+5=6
		2+1=3	3+1=4	4+1=5	5+1=6
			2+2=4	2+3=5	2+4=6
				3+2=5	4+2=6
					3+3=6

We learned that lizard 1 could never leap. We learned that lizards 6, 7, and 8 would win most of the time.

Can you see why?

	8	9	10	11	12
-6=7	2+6=8	3+6=9	4+6=10	5+6=11	6+6=12
-1=7	6+2=8	6+3=9	6+4=10	6+5=11	
+5=7	3+5=8	4+5=9	5+5=10		
+2=7	5+3=8	5+4=9			
-4=7	4+4=8				
-3=7					

Glossary

cube: a solid shape that has six square sides.

finish line: the place where a race or a game ends.

leap: to jump.

roll: in a game, to shake and toss number cubes.

space: a square on a game board.

starting line: the place to begin a race or a game.

Index